CELEBRATE AROUND THE YEAR

by Meish Goldish

Harcourt
SCHOOL PUBLISHERS

D1797536

ISBN 10: 0-15-350320-3
ISBN 13: 978-0-15-350320-7

Ordering Options
ISBN 10: 0-15-349941-9 (Grade 6 ELL Collection)
ISBN 13: 978-0-15-349941-8 (Grade 6 ELL Collection)
ISBN 10: 0-15-357366-X (package of 5)
ISBN 13: 978-0-15-357366-8 (package of 5)

5 6 7 8 9 10   0940   12 11 10 09

Washington, D.C., the capital of the United States, is more than just home to our President and lawmakers. This city is also where dozens of colorful festivals take place every year. The events celebrate people, places, and things of interest and importance to Americans.

In January, some of the many events in the capital commemorate the birthday of Dr. Martin Luther King, Jr. He believed in equal human rights for everyone. Music and film programs honor the life of this leader. You can hear a reading of King's famous "I Have a Dream" speech at the Smithsonian Museum of Natural History.

Do you like parades? Then you might visit Washington, D.C., in February. That's when the Chinese New Year Parade takes place. It's a street celebration that includes dragon dancers in colorful costumes. You'll also find marching bands and Chinese entertainers.

Presidents' Day honors our presidents in February. One parade honors our first president, George Washington. This parade is held just outside the capital, in Alexandria, Virginia.

You can remember Abraham Lincoln by visiting the Lincoln Memorial in Washington, D.C. There you'll hear a reading of Lincoln's famous Civil War speech, the Gettysburg Address.

Do you love animals? Then March is a great time to be in Washington, D.C. That's when the Smithsonian National Zoo holds its North American Wildlife Celebration. You can view a live bald eagle, our national bird. You can also see sea lions, wolves, otters, and other popular North American creatures.

The zoo festival includes many hands-on displays. There are animal programs to help you learn and have fun!

In March and April, people in Washington, D.C., enjoy the National Cherry Blossom Festival. This event celebrates the 3,000 cherry trees that the city of Tokyo gave our nation's capital. In the spring, the trees blossom with beautiful pink and white flowers. They brighten the entire area along the Potomac River.

The festival doesn't end with the cherry trees. There are also street shows, parades, outdoor concerts, and fireworks. In addition, there's the popular Smithsonian Kite Festival. Kids make kites and compete in kite-flying contests.

An old joke says that sheep get haircuts at the "baa-baa shop." A barbershop is where people can get their hair cut. You can see real sheep get their wool removed at Mount Vernon's "Sheep Get a Haircut" celebration. It's held every May in Mount Vernon, Virginia, just outside Washington, D.C. Visitors watch as the wool is shaved off the sheep. People also learn about the sheep that once grazed on George Washington's farm.

Perhaps you'd rather be in outer space in May? Then visit Space Day at the Smithsonian National Air and Space Museum. There you can meet real astronauts and hear them talk about their space adventures.

Would you like to travel the globe without going into space? Then the Smithsonian Folklife Festival is for you. This celebration is held in June and July on the National Mall. It celebrates traditions of different peoples around the world.

There are dance and music programs from many countries. Storytellers tell tales from many different parts of the world. You can see crafts that come from each country. You can even taste foods that are popular in each land.

July is a special month in Washington. The Fourth of July marks the birthday of the United States of America. You can expect lots of excitement at the Fourth of July fireworks displays. Gather on the National Mall in downtown Washington, D.C. This mall does not have stores. It is a large strip of parkland. See blazing fireworks light up the sky!

July isn't just about fireworks. You can enjoy a musical performance on Independence Day in Mount Vernon. General George Washington—or at least someone dressed just like him—pays a visit. You can even eat free birthday cake!

August is a great time to be outdoors around Washington, D.C. Many summer fairs take place in towns in Maryland and Virginia. They offer everything from carnival rides to animal shows. Don't forget the musical programs and arts and crafts displays, too!

Do you prefer historical displays? Then enjoy the Maryland Renaissance Festival in Crownsville, Maryland. Visit a sixteenth-century village. See crafts and games from 400 years ago.

September is about returning to school. A great way to prepare is by attending the National Book Festival in Washington, D.C. You'll find authors reading from their works on the National Mall. Perhaps your favorite writer will be there!

September is also the month when the United States Constitution was signed. This famous paper sets forth our country's basic laws. You can view the Constitution in the National Archives Building in Washington, D.C. You'll find the Declaration of Independence and the Bill of Rights there, too.

Is fall your favorite season? Then you'll like the fall festivals held in October in the Washington, D.C. area. You can go on a hayride or pick a pumpkin from a patch.

One of the biggest festivals is the Harvest Festival in Derwood, Maryland. There you can make your own scarecrow out of hay! If you really love hay, get lost in the Hay Maze, and then try to find your way out!

In November, our nation's capital observes two important holidays. Veterans Day honors those who have served in the military for the United States. In Washington, D.C., special ceremonies are held at several memorials. They include the Vietnam Memorial and the Navy Memorial.

Later in the month, people celebrate Thanksgiving with lively parades. The Montgomery County Annual Thanksgiving Parade includes giant balloons! Colorful floats and marching bands are also there. Floats are displays on wheels that people have made for a parade.

December may bring snow to our nation's capital. However, the spirit of America stays warm. Free holiday celebrations for kids take place at the National Zoo. People can view live animals and a variety of arts and crafts. Be sure to see the musical theater shows, too!

Now we've reached the end of the year. You may not live in Washington, D.C. However, if you do get a chance to visit, you'll surely enjoy it. Our nation's capital has many festivals and celebrations. There's something for everyone!

Scaffolded Language Development

USING PREPOSITIONAL PHRASES Tell students that a prepositional phrase is a short phrase that includes a preposition, the object of the preposition (a noun or a pronoun), and any words that modify the object such as *a* or *the*. Have students look for the following prepositional phrases in the text:

in the capital
at the Smithsonian Museum of Natural History
along the Potomac River
on George Washington's farm
on the National Mall

Have students use the above phrases to complete the following sentences.

1. United States lawmakers work _____.
2. You can see and hear various exhibits _____.
3. Many different vegetables were grown _____.
4. The Smithsonian Folklife Festival takes place _____.
5. Every day many people walk and run _____.

 ## Social Studies

Holidays Ask students to name the different holidays they know. Write their responses on the chalkboard. Have students tell what each holiday commemorates and how it is celebrated.

School-Home Connection

 **School-Home Connection** Have students share the information in this book with family members. Then have family members imagine a new festival and how the festival would be celebrated.

Word Count: 976